# DEAR LOVE,

*The Cycle of a Situationship*

## J. A. BUIE

*Artwork & Illustrations by*
GORDON PYE

Indigo Inked Publishing Services

Copyright © 2018 by J. A. Buie

All rights reserved.

No part of this book may be reproduced in any form or by any electronic or mechanical means, including information storage and retrieval systems, without written permission from the author, except for the use of brief quotations in a book review.

ISBN: 978-0-578-40756-2

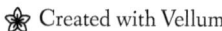 Created with Vellum

*Written & Edited by:* J. A. Buie
*Website: www.byjabuie.com*
*Email: jabuie@byjabuie.com*
*Instagram: @the_jabuie*
*Facebook: JA Buie The WritHer*
*Twitter: @the_jabuie*

*Artwork & Illustrations by: Gordon Pye*
*Email: Gordonpyefineart@gmail.com*
*Instagram: @poppi_gordo*

*Cover design by: Dynasty Media Group*
*Email:dynastymediasd@gmail.com*
*www.dynastymedia.net*

*To every young woman out there that has lost
herself in the pursuit of love,
if no one ever told you that love and loyalty
starts with what you give yourself,
I'm telling you now.
I pray you begin to find yourself
among the pages of this book.
Best of Love,
J*

*baby girl,
there's no one in this world that's doper than you
they're open to you
more focused on you
your shine, your spirit, everything about you
try as they may, there will never be another quite like you.
-J. A. Buie*

CONTENT:

- the beginning- lusting for love
- the middle- flashing lights
- the end- reality check
- beginning again- the epiphany
- excerpt- Dear Daddy, An Open Letter to An Absentee Father- A Memoir

**the beginning**

**lusting for love**

* * *

# LUSTING FOR LOVE

The beginning is always the same, short and sweet. They meet you, they court you, they make you feel like you're just the sweetest thing to them, no Lauryn Hill. Everything is fresh and fun like the first day of Spring. Of course, you have suspicions in the beginning like you always do when you meet someone new, it's natural. These days a new guy equals new drama, but you remain optimistic. The only other option is to be leery, and this time you just want to have a little hope in something. He could be different after all, he could be the one this time. So your guard and your walls are down and all of the rules and stipulations you usually apply are casually hung up in your closet next to your favorite winter pea coat. In a matter of weeks, days even, you both seem to be professing your infatuated feelings for each other with cute little text message check-ins throughout the day, and it's not long before the kissy face and heart emoji's follow. He checks almost every box on your "perfect guy" check list and for the most part you can see yourself with him. You just pray that the feelings are mutual and whatever this is you two are doing, you're doing together. There's potential here and it's worth exploring, but in order to get there, you have to play his game. You have to show him that you're the one. That you're worth the leap of faith and that you can and will be everything he needs and more. He just doesn't quite see it yet and that's fine, because you see it enough for the both of you. So you begin this pursuit of going after what you want. Why not right? Balls to the walls and all, you will get your guy by any means necessary. So you do all of the things you believe a good catch is supposed to do. You answer within the first two to three rings when he calls, you're cooking for him, sleeping pretty next to him, and asking him about his dreams, fears, goals and where he sees his self in the next couple of years. You begin submerging yourself further and further into him searching for that special connection, that thing you feel will bring him closer to you. But in the midst of you embarking on this mission to attain love everlasting, you missed something. You missed a BIG something. You missed the part where he still wants to pursue other options while you pursue him, and of course he doesn't want to give up the benefits of being your only pursuant. He also isn't going to be honest with you about it and give you the option to bow out gracefully. Too easy. So you hear things come out of his mouth like, "I mean you know what it is with us" and "Why do we need a title to explain what we are to everyone else, we know what WE ARE!" At times he may even lead you to believe that he's cool with you having other friends too, but he isn't and he will never be. So it's agreed, this is a thing, without a title. My dear, this is not a relationship, you've just entered into a situationship. Let the journey begin.

dear love,

i like you

i'm infatuated by you

you make me smile

it's been a while since that's happened

since someone's made me smile the way that you do

who are you?

who sent you and where did you come from?

i'm intrigued by you.

dear love,

my phone was in my lap when you called

either the vibration setting on it was set so high

that it traveled through my dress

penetrated my skin

and crawled into my stomach wall

or those were butterflies.

dear love,

please don't be another fuckboy.

dear love,

the more time i spend getting to know you

the more i see you in my life

i know that life is full of firsts'

but i feel like this first time

will be the last

i feel like you

could be my one.

dear love,

the idea of you and i looks so promising

your consistency gives me hope

you're different from anyone i've ever known

and well

that's refreshing.

dear love,

that first night

our eyes danced on each other's bodies to a tune only we knew

our hands intertwined our fingers like wild vines

our lips pursed against each other's

forcing our tongues to dance a jig

your touch soft and subtle up my spine

firm, yet still delicate

while gripping my waist

after i made love to you

i wandered to myself

will he be as gentle with my heart

as he is with my body?

dear love,

let's recreate little versions of each other.

dear love,
in my head
our wedding day is near
the dress, the cake, the venue, and honeymoon are all planned
i've already picked kitchen tile and accent walls
for our big house on the hill
i've birthed our children, named them
and enrolled them in the best private schools
he looks just like you, and she just like me
we go on romantic getaways some weekends
to keep our love hot and heavy
and long family vacays to places like
Santorini, Seychelles and Maldives
you treat me like royalty and i put no one above you
our bond is like none other
picture perfect love, right?
is our future as clear to you
as it is to me?

dear love,

you look like forever to me.

dear love,

how can you be the reason my heart beats and stops

all at the same time?

dear love,

what are you afraid of?

why won't you let me in?

have i not shown you that i'm enough?

that you need not look anywhere else

i know that you know what you've had

but do you know what you could have?

i can be any and everything you need me to be

if you just let me in

won't you just let me in?

dear love,

you send me "Good Morning" text

but you only invite me over after midnight

is my love not good enough for you

in the daylight?

dear love,

if you ever find yourself between myself and another woman

choose her

i don't compete for spots in people's lives

and love isn't a contest

these days i have no problem losing by forfeit.

dear love,

i'm not interested in being just another number in your phone

another "gm beautiful" to add to your list of text

to send every morning

you pass those out like Halloween candy

but i think you should know

i don't do tricks for treats.

dear love,

i am not a game

do not play me.

**the middle**

**flashing lights**

* * *

# FLASHING LIGHTS

Much time has passed in your new situationship. So much time that it's become comfortable to you and you've become loyal to it. The mere thought of starting over now just drains your soul. Feelings have grown strong and deep, and like a 401k plan after the first couple of years, you're now fully vested. Funny part about having feelings is that it seems like they always develop right before the bright yellow flashing lights appear. Yellow flashing lights are your warning. Yellow flashing lights mean PUMP YOUR BREAKS, DO NOT PASS GO, DO NOT COLLECT $200! These are the signs warning you that a person really may not be who they betrayed themselves to be in the beginning. Yes he may have made you feel like you were the only one, but he wasn't being honest with you. The picking up after two to three rings is long gone. Nowadays you're getting his voicemail way more often than you would like, and those missed calls don't get returned until hours later, sometimes the next day even. Leaving your mind plagued with questions and self-assumed answers of his whereabouts and who's keeping him company. You've cried yourself to sleep many nights wondering where you went wrong and why he just isn't giving you more of his time and attention. When you aren't crying, your up all night consuming yourself with a bunch of what if scenarios, it's crazy. When you finally do get that call back it's a lame excuse about falling asleep early, having to work late, his phone going dead and blah blah blah. Any challenge you place to his excuse you're made to feel as if you are the one that did something wrong because your being too needy, too nagging or just not trusting enough. Next thing you know, you're apologizing to him. CRAZY RIGHT!? On top of all of that you have this little nuisance of a voice in your head convincing you that staying in this situation, battling your feelings for someone that may not even really be worth your time and energy in the long run is better than starting over with someone new. Or worse, being alone again. So what do you do? You stay. I know my dear it has happened to the best of us, and if you don't recognize it by now, this is the cycle. The toxic, unhealthy, draining, never-ending, everlasting cycle of a situationship. It just goes around and around and up and down over and over again. Much unlike those theme park roller coasters though, this one only ends when you decide to get off. My only advice at this point, is to ride the wave.

dear love,

you say you love me

but do you really?

because while i hear your words

my mind is stuck on the text messages i stumbled across

in your phone last night

from the un-saved number

that a had a text thread way too long

of encrypted and coded words and emoji's

to just be

nobody.

dear love,

no more chances.

dear love,

you breathe life into me and suffocate me

all at the same time

most days i can't tell if i'm coming or going

i'm high when i'm with you

but when you're gone

i can't tell which way is up from down

my flesh feels alive

but my soul is slowly dying.

dear love,

because i see potential in every single apology

and have hope in every broken promise you make

i always believe that this time

is the time you'll actually make the change

so i stay.

dear love,

i swear i'm done this time.

dear love,

i crave and fear you

i crave the sunshine you provide on those days

when skies are gray

but i fear the damage to my eyes your sun rays bring

when i'm around you too long

you leave me too blind to see the truth of who you are

or maybe it's that very truth that blinds me

maybe my truth is

your truth i just don't want to see.

dear love,

this gray area we seem to be in

this area of it's "undefined" but you're mine

this area of "no lies allowed" let's keep it real

you never express yourself

you say i should already know how you feel

but i'm not a mind reader

this isn't what i signed up for

on the fly, yeah i fuck with you

even though deep down i know i deserve more

it's been too many years and not enough effort

a lot of finger pointing and judgements passed

secrets unfolded lines crossed and feelings tainted

we let go but we come right back

so this is my dilemma

with this gray area i no longer have a stance

it's either black or white

are we in or are we out

because i can no longer do this dance.

dear love,

i'm a first round draft pick, period

you don't want me on your team?

cool

just don't come back later for the trade up

unlike the game of basketball

my love is not up for negotiations.

dear love,

while you were out

busy collecting stones

you neglected the diamond

you had at home.

dear love,

i'm such a fool

every time you call or text

i conveniently forget the pain you've caused only hours before

and succumb to my need for comfort and pleasure

how both idiotic and oxymoronic of me to seek refuge

in the very same person that caused me strife.

dear love,

i promised myself i would never cry for you again

but here i am

pillow soaked from the hurricane of tears

that just won't stop flowing.

dear love,

the truth only hurts temporarily

i can heal from that and move on

the lie hurts forever

because you didn't think enough of me to tell me the truth.

dear love,

you don't get credit for your intentions,

you get credit for your actions.

dear love,

no matter how hard i try

the woman i am

will never be able to please the boy you are.

dear love,

how could you betray me when i needed you most?

how could you just throw my love away?

how dare you think you were the prize in this relationship

how funny of you to think that after all of that

i would stay.

dear love,

i'm glutton for your agony

i approve of the heartache you bring

i invite tears with open arms to lay on my pillow at night

i yearn for emptiness to fill my heart yet again

i commence to keep running back to you

and of course each time you let me in

because it's quite evident

that the only pleasure I've ever known

is the pain you bring.

dear love,

i tried to be all that i could be for you

and everything i thought you needed me to be

i dimmed my light so you could shine

i sacrificed who i was so that we could be

i tried to break into those places

you wouldn't let me in willingly

i took care of your needs and put you first

but you neglected to do the same for me

i tried to get through to you so many times

but my heart, you just couldn't see

now it's time for me to fall out of love with you

and to fall for once

in love with me.

dear love,

just because we've been together forever

doesn't mean we're supposed to be together forever.

dear love,

maybe we should go our separate ways

you know

you do you

i'll do me

'cause we're not doing each other equally.

**the end**

**reality check**

\* \* \*

# REALITY CHECK

The dust has settled and the realizations are beginning to set in. It's becoming more and more clear that you just can't do this shit anymore! You've tried to be patient, but your patience has run thin. You've tried to be understanding, but some things are just beyond your understanding, no matter how hard you try. You've been loving and compassionate, but it felt like all you got in return was taken for granted. He just doesn't see you for who you are. He doesn't see your value, he doesn't see your worth, and he doesn't see that you are more than enough for him. The games have grown old. You know the lies are coming before they even get a chance to exit his lips and creep letter by letter into your ear. He's completely oblivious to how you feel, not because he doesn't care about you, but because he cares about his own feelings, ego and pride so much more. He's used to the threats of you being done because you seem to have been done every other week for the past year. He's used to you ignoring his calls and texts every couple of days and then falling right back into his arms and bed. This isn't new to him. In his mind, you've allowed him to do the things that he's done to you for so long that he's comfortable with this situationship cycle and pattern he's built with you. And hear me when I say he isn't looking to make any changes to it anytime soon. The change is all on you. This situationship cycle won't end until you end it. But this time it's truly different, for you at least. You're finally sick and tired of being sick and tired and change doesn't usually come until you've reached that point. Don't be confused my dear, this is a very good place to be. Unfortunately it isn't the end, just yet.

dear love,

day one is always the hardest.

dear love,

sometimes you just have to wake up

look yourself in the mirror and say,

" *I deserve better than this*".

dear love,

he said i looked like the type to wife

but he had no intentions of doing so

he wanted the benefits of me

without being committed to me

he wanted my love, my sex, my loyalty

but he really could've cared less for me

he gave me his free time

you know

his in between time

in the mean time

but when i needed him his time he couldn't free up for me

when i would ask him just what this was

he never could answer me

i gave him everything he asked for

but he couldn't give hisself to me

now i'm gone and he wants me back

he begs for time that i don't have

says now he'll have a relationship with me

but it's too late

because now i'm committed to me.

dear love,

i was chasing you

you were chasing her

she was chasing him

we were all chasing someone

who was chasing someone else.

dear love,

my world didn't begin with you

and i refuse to let it end with you

dear love,

i didn't give up on you

i just don't care to be played for a fool anymore.

dear love,

when you told me you didn't want to do this anymore

i felt that

truth of the matter is

i didn't want to either

i just didn't want to be the first to say it.

dear love,

this is a reminder that sometimes you just gotta go ghost

no text

no phone calls

turn the read receipts off

he'll get the picture when he doesn't hear from you

no need to explain.

dear love,

i used my time, my energy and sacrificed my heart

to build you up

only for you to tear me down.

dear love,

it only took me a day to fall for your charm

but years to fall out of your web of lies.

dear love,

i find it quite odd how when you don't call my phone

i feel both anxiety and relief

it's scary to know there's a part of me

that still wants to hear from you

but it feels to good to know that for the most part

i'm getting over you.

dear love,

i was trying to mend the hole in your heart

and didn't even realize

i was gaining one in mine.

dear love,

i longed for you

i was in search of you

i thought i had you

silly of me.

dear love,

you were careless with my love

you weren't deserving of who i was

you stopped pretending to care

and your words no longer matched your actions

the things that were once fuzzy to me

have become so crystal clear

the vision i once saw of us

no longer exist.

dear love,

i miss the hell out of you

but i'll never give you the satisfaction of knowing it.

dear love,

i believed the lies you told me were true

i believed them because i believed in me and you

i believed that you would change for me one day

now i believe the only person that lost something

from this relationship

was you.

dear love,

you said things to me that you didn't mean

to get things from me that you didn't deserve.

dear love,

i spread my legs for you

and out poured my soul

another piece of me sacrificed

for nothing in return.

dear love,

i fell in love with the soul of you

but your ego got in the way.

dear love,

i don't negotiate with egos.

dear love,

i now know where i went wrong

i was trying to be everything

to someone who was looking for nothing.

dear love,

it was so easy for me to let you in

yet so hard for me to let you go.

dear love,

i really thought we had something

i guess now we'll never know.

dear love,

from time to time i catch myself

wondering what it could've been between us

what we could've had

who we could've been to each other

but none of that would've ever been

because you were just another artful deception

you were all smoke and mirrors.

dear love,

i should've walked away when i met you

i should've never given you my number that day

but my eyes saw forever written in your smile

all the while

my mind was whispering *"he looks like another mistake"*

dear love,

it was fun while it lasted.

**beginning again**

**the epiphany**

\* \* \*

# THE EPIPHANY

Now that you've had time to mourn the loss of this man and the situationship, it's time to move on. You've beat yourself up again and again over all of the reasons the situationship had to end and why all the parts you played in it led to it's demise. You no longer have the urge to call, text, drive by his house, or show up at events or outings that you know he'll be at just to "bump into him". You don't even care if he miraculously changes into a whole new man and does right by the next woman, because he's no longer a loss in your eyes. You are okay with everything exactly as it happened and exactly how it ended because all of that was necessary to get to this exact point right here, loving you and being open to a new healthy love. You've learned your lesson and you've finally gotten to a place where you no longer care to point fingers and place blame. You've had time to reflect on you and see that you are truly worth more than you allow yourself to settle for, and my love, you were settling. You are in a much better place. You can now look back and acknowledge that maybe, just maybe that situation wasn't for you and that man was not the one for you. The love that's meant for you will come, and I promise you that it will not come with games, lies, deceit, blurred lines or undefined titles. It won't be a challenge and it won't be so hard because my dear love isn't supposed to be that hard. It will be real and everything you ever dreamed of. If in the demise of your relationship, you find yourself holding on to feelings of regret, anger and vengeance, then that relationship needed to come to an end. Relationships are meant to teach us about ourselves. Through our interactions and exchanges with other people, we learn more about who we are and what we want in life. Take only what you need from the situation and use it to build a better you, not a bitter you. But in the meantime and in between time, just love on you.

dear love,

i have my mother's thighs

and my father's smile

both a gift and a curse

both a blessing

my mother taught me

how not to let a man treat you

not to degrade you

or walk all over you

not to cheat or beat on you

or expose your insecurities

because i watched men do all of those things to her

and still i allowed them to do those things to me

my father taught me

that when a man loves you

when he truly loves you

he will never leave you

he will fight to the ends of the earth to protect you

he will honor you

and he will cherish you

all of these things my father didn't do for me

and even though he left me

i still know that he loved me

all of these things i learned

from my mother's thighs

and my father's smile.

Inspired by Warsan Shire's *I have my mother's mouth*

dear love,

when Drake said,

"...had a man last year life goes on."

i felt that.

dear love,

you walked into a horse stable

and picked yourself out a unicorn

lucky you

but where you went wrong was

when you expected me to gallop like the rest

my dear

didn't you know i could fly?

dear love,

it wasn't a soft spot that i had for you

it was a false hope that kept you in my life

longer than you should've been.

dear love,

i was never hungry for you

but my insecurities were starving.

dear love,

from the worst parts of you

i was able to improve the best parts of me.

dear love,

i want to be in a relationship where ego's

and insecurities don't exist.

dear love,

never again will i give all of me

for pieces of someone else.

dear love,

you tried to weaken me

but you only made me stronger.

dear love,

i was attempting to do the impossible with you

trying to get you to love me

the way that i loved you

was like

chasing sunsets and draining oceans.

dear love,

pain can be pleasure

but it can never be love.

dear love,

i'm just in a different space

in a different place

that's all.

dear love,

if the attraction isn't equal

if the effort isn't matched

if the feelings aren't mutual

if true emotions aren't attached

then i don't want it.

dear love,

don't ever settle for me

because i will never settle for you.

dear love,

you were just another lesson

i needed to learn.

dear love,

at the end of the day

we are all just broken pieces

looking to be made whole.

dear love,

my worth was always there

it may have been hidden among my flaws and insecurities

but it was there

maybe it was just that

it wasn't for you to see

maybe it was just that

spiritually it knew you couldn't afford

a woman like me.

# DEAR DADDY
AN OPEN LETTER TO AN ABSENTEE FATHER

Dear Daddy,

They say the first love of a little girl should be the love of her father. The daddy-daughter bond is is the most sought after relationship in the world by a woman. Having a father is viable in a young woman's life from her very first baby booties to her first pair of Louboutins. The absence or presence of a father at a young age sets the precedence for a little girl's future relationships with the many people of the world that she will encounter in her life, men and women alike. As the first man in her life, a daddy's job is to show his baby girl the way a woman is supposed to be loved, adored and cherished by a man. Swooning over her every coooo and kick when she's fresh out the womb and right by her side with every pedal stroke she takes her first time without training wheels on her pretty pink princess bike. As an adolescent, he is supposed to show her what it feels like to be treated and spoiled by a man. Like buying her her very first charm bracelet for receiving all A's on her report card, or purchasing her very first car for her sweet $16^{th}$ birthday. Then maintaining the care of the car for her, oil changes, tune-ups and tire rotations to ensure her safety out on the roads. As a woman, he is there to show her what is to be expected and accepted by a man. Like being a provider and protector for his family and loving, caring for and respecting his wife, the Queen of the castle and mother of his children. Through this relationship between a father and a daughter, the little girl also learns what it feels like to love a man unconditionally. She understands what it is like to have a man in her life, to care and look after her and keep her safe from harm. He supports, uplifts and guides her through those times in life when only a Daddy's touch will provide the answer. He makes her feel like she is the most beautiful person in the world every chance he gets. He is the first man to ever dance with her, buy her flowers and wipe her tears when they fall. Having a father in her life gives that little girl a confidence about herself. A confidence that lets her know that she can do, be and have anything on this earth her little heart desires and that when she falls, he will be right there by her side to catch her and soothe her woes. When she has had a father in her life, she knows her value and her worth down to the cent and she won't settle for anything less than full price. She knows that she is precious, like a diamond in the rough and she knows that when a man loves her, when he truly loves her, she will never ever have to second-guess his love for her. His love for her is unconditional and there is nothing in the world she would ever have to do to be deserving of that love, other than be who God put her on this green earth to be. She knows that she is enough, always has been and always will be.

You walked out of my life long before I got the chance to blow out the candles on my second birthday cake, leaving my mother to be another single parent. You two were pretty young and immature, still green to the world and all that it entailed. Mom was only 15 years old when she got pregnant with me. An insecure chubby little city girl still lost and finding herself. The third oldest child of five children by grandmother's third baby-father. My grandmother was the only child of my great-grandmother, so my mother and aunt and uncle had no cousins. My great grandmother was an only child as well, so my grandmother and her siblings had no cousins either. After my great grandmother had my grandmother, she took a break from child-bearing before having her next three children along side her daughter's first three children. They were all born so close together, they grew up like cousins instead of aunts, uncles, nieces and nephews. Our matriarchal family, headed by my great grandmother was majority women. Women having and raising babies without any real father figures to help pick up the slack or support us. The few men we did have in the family, well, they were present but that's as far as it went.

From what I do know of your upbringing, it was very different than that of my mother's. You were the youngest of three to the same mother and father in the same home. You were shipped off from your home town of Monroe, Louisiana when you joined the Navy and ended up getting stationed in San Diego, California where you met my mother and created me. You grew up with your brother and sister in the south, and had cousins and aunts and uncles and fathers. You actually had fathers in your village. Imagine that. Men staying around to have multiple children with one woman and cultivate families. On my mother's side, I can count with two fingers how many women had more than two children by the same father. I learned early on that the concept of family holds more weight in the south than it does on the west coast.

I never really heard your version of the story on how you and my mother met. My mother said she was headed to meet up with one of her girlfriends at Balboa Park next to the zoo one Saturday. Apparently in the 80's, it was the popular hangout spot for young military guys like yourself. In San Diego, where ever the young sailors hung out, the young women in the city were sure to flock to. Marrying a military man was the closest thing to marrying an NFL star for a San Diego women. It was considered a mil ticket, without the mil, but a ticket to a somewhat decent life nonetheless. If a woman was lucky enough to land a man with not just gainful employment, but a career and making a decent income plus benefits, you could get out of the hood. San Diego is a beautiful city to visit, palm trees and sunshine for miles. Tourist coming in and out all seasons long, but if you travel far enough inland, east of the beaches, it gets a little tougher, a little rougher, a little realer. Clearly, my mother wasn't one of those lucky woman and the relationship between you and her would be nothing more than meeting each other that day, hooking up about two weeks later, hanging out a time or two after that, a deployment, a pregnancy and the birth of your first and only daughter together. It's funny how temporary situations can produce a lifetime connection between two people. You probably didn't know this, but Grandma told my mother the first time she met you that you weren't the one for her, I guess Grandma was right. Mothers know best.

I was born on a Friday, January 25$^{th}$, 1985, a winter baby. You were out to sea finishing up a Westpac deployment on the USS Schenectady. My mother said you returned back a few days after I was born and came to see me. I was a spitting image of you and as much as it pains me to admit it, I still look so much like you. I'm sure that you had all of those thoughts, visions and dreams of what a relationship with your first born daughter would be like and all of the things you planned to do with me as I grew up and blossomed into a beautiful young lady, but I guess life got in the way. You never got the chance to become that father. We didn't take walks in the park with me licking an ice cream cone and sitting up on your shoulders in the spring time. You didn't get to kiss my first boo-boo when I fell at the beach playground in the summer, and you weren't there to show me how to ride my first pink bike without training wheels after school in the fall. You didn't buy me my first charm bracelet or my first car. If I'm being honest, I can't tell you that I remember a lot that you have done for me in life since I was born. I know this is going to be hard but my first memories of who my father was, were not of you. They were of a boyfriend that my mother dated shortly after you left. For now, we'll just call him Avery. I absolutely adored Avery, and Avery adored me. I thought for the better part of my childhood that Avery truly was my father. At one point his face was the one I envisioned whenever I dreamed or wandered about my father, but I think it was just because I was too young when you left to really remember who you were. By the time Avery came around, well I guess my memory bank just kept a photo of his face. Avery was tall, dark, bald and handsome. Just my mother's type. He had a gorgeous smile with dimples and his teeth were perfect, white and straight. Like you, Avery was in the Navy too. According to my mother the first time Avery came over to my grandmother's house to meet me, I was sitting in the front yard eating a popsicle and when he walked through the front gate, I yelled, "Daddy" and jumped into his arms. We were inseparable from that day on. In hindsight, I see that that was my first cry for your love. I was so young, only two, yet I knew someone important was missing from my life.

From time to time, Avery would borrow a friend's car and come and pick me up from my grandmother's house and we would drive around the city. He would take me with him to run his errands and take me to his job with him sometimes. I loved that car. It was a gold Nissan 300zx with a T-Top sunroof. I swore to myself when I was old enough to drive, that would be my first car. When I was with Avery, to anyone that asked, I was his daughter. Even though the relationship between my mother and Avery was short lived, as some of her future relationships would be in the years to come, my memories of Avery have stayed with me all this time. One memory in particular was of a Halloween we spent together. My mother was too tired or too lazy to take me Trick-or-Treating in the apartment complex where we lived. I remember it was our first apartment we moved into after we moved out of my grandmother's house. If my memory serves me correctly, I was a princess that year. The costume came complete with a plastic tiara and a shiny plastic silver scepter to match. Avery and I got in the car and drove up the hill from our apartment complex to the 7-Eleven right on the corner by the bus stop where the winos, pimps and drug dealers dwelled. We walked in the store and I made a bee line straight to the candy aisle. Avery let me pick out as much candy as I wanted. Now-n-Laters, Blow Pops, Bazooka Joe Gum, Red Hots, Lemonheads, Laffy Taffy, Sugar Daddy's, Whatchamacallits and anything else I could hold onto in my five year old arms. I remember the store cashier looking down at me from the other side of the counter and saying in a thick but comprehendible accent, "Somebody's going to have a lot of cavities after tonight! I wish my Dad would have taken me to the store and let me pick out my own candy for Halloween when I was little. What a lucky little girl you are to have a dad like him." I just looked up at him, smiled and nodded my head in a yes motion waiting patiently for him to finish ringing us up. The cashier placed my Halloween treats in a brown paper bag, the ones they give the winos to hide their 40 ounce bottles in, and handed them to me. I looked to Avery for the okay to remove a piece right away and once he gave me the head nod, I reached for the watermelon Larry Taffy. Watermelon is still my favorite candy flavor to this day. My favorite part of the taffy candy were the black edible sees stuck to the top of it to the portray the inside of a real watermelon. I was too elated! I had just gotten a bag full of full size candy for Halloween and didn't have to go and knocking door to door to get it. No fun size miniature candy bars for me this year. My little friends in the apartment complex down the hill were so jealous when I got back and showed them what kind of Halloween night I had. Avery pulled out his wallet, paid the cashier and out the door to the car we headed. He always opened my door first and made sure my seatbelt was buckled securely. I probably should have been sitting in the back seat, but Avery said that was for little girls, and I was a big girl, so he let me ride shotgun for the minute and a half drive back down the hill to our apartment. Nothing and no one could take away my smile at that moment. Avery in the driver seat, my petite little five year-old frame sunk into the passenger seat with my twig legs dangling above the car floor. Avery looked over at me from the driver seat. He smiled that Colgate smile and asked,

"You good babygirl?"

"Yep, I'm good."

"Alright then, let's roll on home to your momma and show her all the good candy you got for Halloween."

I had a bag full of candy in my lap, my pink princess costume on, and the beautiful California sun setting above us. I can still see the sky through the t-top of that gold Nissan 300zx. I can still taste that first bite of watermelon taffy and the crunch of the faux watermelon seeds. I can still see Avery sitting behind the steering wheel with his burgundy velour sweatsuit on and sunglasses tilted on top of his shining bald head. This was a bond. This was love. This was supposed to be us. The love and bond between a daddy and a daughter, and a relationship I would spend the next 26 years of my life in search of.

- An Exercept from J.A.Buie's upcoming memoir:

*Dear Daddy- An Open Letter to an Absentee Father*

www.ingramcontent.com/pod-product-compliance
Lightning Source LLC
Chambersburg PA
CBHW051358290426
44108CB00015B/2072